MANLY GOLF

50 Ways to Muscle Your Way to Victory

Chris Rodell

Illustrations by Peter Georgeson

**Andrews McMeel
Publishing**

Kansas City

Manly Golf is produced by becker&mayer!, Bellevue, Washington.
www.beckermayer.com

Edited by Ben Raker
Designed by Katie LeClercq
Production management by Cindy Curren

To Paul Rodell, the manliest golfer I know.
Thanks, Dad, for all the mulligans.

Section 1:

BE PREPARED

THE RIGHT TOOLS FOR THE JOB

Get a Tattoo

Nothing says commitment like a tattoo. One golf tattoo is good, two is better, but a whole bunch—prominently displayed—is best. Eventually, you'll want to cover yourself with so many tattoos that it looks like you're wearing a really tight print shirt. That way, even courses that don't allow players to golf shirtless will let you play. Become the Dennis Rodman of golf. Mix gothic tats, like the grim reaper driving a souped-up golf cart across your forehead, with historic ones, such as a complete list of every golfer who's won the British Open Championship. Insist that the tattoo artist include the unabridged rules of golf on some meaty part of your body, preferably a buttock, so you can conveniently drop your trousers to settle disputes.

▶ **Result:** Four strokes added to the scores of distracted opponents. They'll spend more time reading you than reading putts. Plus, every rule dispute will go your way as no one will want to stare at your butt to discern the finer points of Article 6A.

What's in a Name?

To get the tee time you want, round up a bunch of golf towels and shove them under your golf shirt so you look like Mr. Universe. When the "McCormick" party is called to the first tee, walk right up to the McCormick group and tell them YOUR name is McCormick too . . . and there's NO QUESTION in your mind that the call is for you, NOT them. One look at your bulging biceps, and they'll practically beg you to start ahead of them.

▶ **Result:** Your score will drop by two strokes. Chances are, if you look like a beefcake, then you'll start to play like one, too.

Quarterback Fake

Let them know you've come to PLAY! Golf is manly, but golf played football-style is even manlier. Prepare by taping a wide Breathe Right strip across the bridge of your nose and smudging nonreflecting black grease under your eyes. No more sun in your eyes as you track the 400-yard pounding you just gave that poor little Titleist. Instead of merely stretching on the first tee, practice throwing your shoulder into a sturdy tee-side oak. The second anyone yells "Fore!" and hits a ball your direction, turn toward the incoming missile and signal a fair catch as your buddies dive for cover behind the cart.

▶ **Result:** Adds two strokes to opponent scores. Give the impression that you think of golf as a contact sport, and you'll have your edge.

12

Be a Real Brut

Prepare by building up a resistance to offensive, eye-stinging vapors. Then, while your opponent is stretching at the first tee, pull out a one-gallon jug of cheap aftershave (possibly spiked with turpentine) and slap handful after handful on your face, neck, chest, and underarms until the entire gallon is dripping from your disintegrating clothing. Your opponent's eyes will water so badly that he'll miss his first tee shot and will be demoralized for the rest of the match.

▶ **Result:** Your opponent's score will increase by at least five strokes. As an added bonus, you'll enjoy your round in perfect silence as all noisy bird and insect life drops to the ground in stunned silence.

Elevate Your Game

Install a jetpack in your over-the-shoulder golf bag. Strap yourself in tight. On the first blind shot to an elevated green, fire that baby up and amaze your partners by rocketing into the sky for an unobstructed view of the hole. For dramatic effect, begin a NASA-style countdown ten seconds prior to liftoff.

▶ **Result**: A personal rocket gives you an incredible advantage assessing the lay of the land. This will take at least three strokes off your score.

Bombs Away

Wear a bandolier of hand grenades across your chest. This stylish look has very practical applications for manly golfers. Any time your ball is within four feet of the hole, toss a grenade nearby so the explosion will bump your ball in. Better yet, use the grenades to make your own holes. Just to make it sporting, hit your ball first and try to guess where it's going to stop. Chuck the grenade five feet past the ball; the ball will drop in the moment a new hole is created. Duck behind the nearest bunker and don't come up until the debris stops raining from the sky.

▶ **Result:** Subtracts one stroke per hole, until you are forcibly removed by the marshal. Opponents may withdraw for medical reasons.

Convict Clothing

Forget about sports shirts with trendy country club logos. Get a standard-issue prison uniform and have a friend you trust fire five bullet holes into it. Be absolutely certain you're not wearing it when the bullets fly.

▶ Result: Other golfers will give you a wide berth if you show up in prison stripes. Besides this, you'll stay cool with the ventilation provided by bullet holes.

20

Tool Time

Can't decide what to carry in your bag? There are really only two clubs you need to play this game: a driver and a putter (and frankly you can get by with just the driver). That means you have room for a number of additional "special-purpose clubs." You might arm yourself with a crossbow, telescopic rifle, and grenade launcher, for starters. If you still feel the need for conventional clubs, at least allow them to be customized. The rules of golf insist you can carry only fourteen clubs in your bag. But they say nothing about club parts. Complete your arsenal with dozens of shafts, grips, and club heads of every size, material, and variety. Go on a hardware-store shopping spree to make sure you have any tool or accessory you'll need to make the game easier.

▶ **Result:** As many strokes off your score as your eraser will allow—who's going to question scorecard "adjustments" made by a guy with a grenade launcher?

Live off the Land

No more hot dogs! Real men catch and kill their own food. Bring along a pocketful of M-80s, light and toss them into the pond, and stun the trout to the surface. Rake them in with your ball retriever, wrap in tin foil, and grill them over the battery of your cart.

▶ **Result:** Five bucks saved by avoiding overpriced halfway house grub. The hearty meal will help you win.

It's All in the Bag

Defy the trend toward lighter, sleeker, more girly golf bags and custom order Bagzilla. Intimidate your foes by lying on your back and bench pressing the fully loaded colossus on the first tee to keep your muscles bulging. Make sure the bag is big enough that you can climb inside it and comfortably wait out storms while your opponents suffer outside your igloo-like golf bag.

▶ **Result:** Since you'll be able to play golf at any time, in any weather (heck, you won't need a home anymore since you can bivouac right on the green), you'll quickly gain the experience you need to give you an edge. Also, since you'll need to transport this thing somehow, you'll finally have a good excuse to buy that monster truck you've had your eye on.

Hey! Beer Man!

Did you know that a standard-size beer keg can be towed around a golf course quite nicely on a pull cart? Well, now you do. And ask yourself this: Would you rather run out of clubs, not having just the right one on hand, or would you rather run out of beer? Case closed. You'll be the most popular guy on the course, and everyone will want you to win. In exchange for free brew, they'll help you find lost balls and will knock your opponents' balls into the trees.

▶ **Result:** Multiple strokes added to your score, but more to opponent scores; plus a really nice buzz for you and your new buddies.

Body-Piercing the Manly Golf Way

The right kind of body-piercing can send a strong statement to your fellow golfers that you are one mean S.O.B. Can you imagine how painful it would look to have a greensman's repair tool pierced through the skin of your nose? What if it were easily removable, allowing you to "rip it out" at every green? Now we're talking manly golf.

▶ **Result:** A completely macho image. Serious intimidation points.

Head Covers with Attitude

Don't you hate those foo-foo club head covers out there? Who the hell wants a cute fluffy bunny or teddy bear head staring at you, as you select your weapon for battle? The manly golfer knows better. Visit your local taxidermist, and on your next outing your club head will be well protected inside the head of a baby croc or in the rear of a raccoon or other roadkill. (Better still, train a live woodland creature to sit on your club head and keep it warm until you bark a command that will signal it to jump off.) Now you're playing with attitude!

▶ Result: Adds four strokes to an opponent's score if you can convince him the raccoon on your driver is alive and rabid.

Light It Up

A flamethrower is very useful on any wooded course. Finesse becomes less essential when the ability to denude hundred-year-old virgin forest growth is "in the bag," so to speak. No need to worry about whether to go over or under that arching branch. Vaporize it! A flamethrower is also helpful on short shots around the green. Rough or scrub grass can be torched away to provide a nice, level surface between you and the cup.

▶ **Result:** Subtracts a minimum of four strokes from your score—more if the course is heavily wooded and you have been following Tip #11.

33

The Spring's the Thing

Spend a night in the workshop installing heavy-duty springs and telescoping shafts into a club. Pull it from the bag the second you hit a ball that lands on a cart path or other ground under repair. The rules state you're allowed "no more than two club lengths" on a free drop. That's when your night's work will bear fruit. Pull the club from your bag and push the button, deploying a club that extends more than twenty yards in any direction. Since you can measure off club lengths using this extra-long club, you'll be able to escape any hazard and legally drop in the middle of any cozy fairway.

▶ Result: Great positioning and about an hour's worth of crybaby moaning from opponents.

Hammer Head

Affix your putter head to the business end of a jackhammer. Use a conventional stroke to start the ball toward the hole. If it looks like it's going to miss, fire up the jackhammer and chase after the ball until the earth-shaking vibrations cause it to drop. Keep the jackhammer running while your opponent shoots—the noise will be so deafening, you will be unable to hear him when he shouts out his score. Just keep shrugging at him when he does this, and write down a snowman for every hole.

▶ **Result:** Subtracts four strokes from your score. Count on adding at least thirty-two strokes to your opponent's score.

Enter the Dragon

Invest in a breakaway T-shirt. Then on your next missed putt, fly into a fists-clenched, vein-popping martial arts frenzy, yell like Bruce Lee, and finish by tearing your shirt in half with one decisive yank. If these antics fail to impress your opponents, proceed by shredding the shirt into confetti-size pieces and then slicing the flag pole in half with a sweeping roundhouse kick. Afterwards, calmly resume play (minus your T-shirt) as if nothing has happened.

▶ **Result:** R-E-S-P-E-C-T. You'll still have missed your putt, but opponents will be sure to leave you space when you line up for your next one.

Section 2:

SHOW THEM WHO'S BOSS

INTIMIDATE OPPONENTS THROUGH SHEER MANLINESS

"T" Time

Play a round dressed like the idol of all manly golfers, Mr. T. Wear so many gold chains around your neck that the simple act of drawing breath rattles the metal enough to distract your jittery opponent. If anyone complains about your behavior, "pity the fool." Then body-slam him off the cart path. Be sure never to utter any sentence longer than four words.

▶ **Result:** Adds three strokes to opponent scores. There's nothing more disconcerting on a golf course than playing against someone like Mr. T.

Manly Golf Tip #18

43

Who's Laughing Now?

"Accidentally" bump the ball off the tee with your driver. When someone jokingly says, "That's one!" fly into a rage about anal rule sticklers, bite the tee in two, rip the carry strap off your golf bag with your teeth, lift and topple the golf cart, toss a few clubs as if they were javelins, and then play the ball from where it lies. Say you understand there are rules and you are happy to obey them, but if the guy wants to be a jerk, fine. After this wild outburst, your rattled opponent will cave hole after hole as you play the round in sullen silence.

▶ **Result:** Adds one stroke to your score, but at least three strokes to the score of your thoroughly frightened opponent.

Blast Away

When it comes to manly golf, most of the action's on the first tee. What happens there sets the tone for the entire round. Therefore, be sure to visit a heavy-duty construction site before each match to buy, trade, or steal industrial blasting caps used to reduce mountains to rubble. Affix one to the face of a dummy driver you don't mind wasting. On the first drive, don protective ear guards and goggles and make a big show of being pumped up. Warn everyone to take a step or two back—for their own safety. Bellow like a gorilla as you take your backswing. The surprise detonation will scare the pants off everyone in your party. Say, "Damn, that happens every time! When am I going to learn to ease off even a little bit?"

▶   Result: Difficult to gauge, but generally, shattered eardrums are very disorienting.

Customized Hog Cart

Now that you're covered in tattoos, it's time to get a ride like a real man—on a customized Harley-Davidson golf cart. Customizing doesn't come cheap, but you need to think of this as a long-term investment in intimidation that is bound to pay off over time. Plus, if you can get all your buddies to pony up for their own Hog Carts, think of the respect you'll command at next Sunday's outing when the starter calls: "Grim Reaper's foursome to the first tee!"

▶ **Result:** Takes four strokes off your score. It's hard not to play like a badass when you've got yourself a Harley.

Big-Time Chest Hair

When it's summer and it's hot, it's time to show off the kind of guy you really are. Start your round with your golf shirt fully buttoned. As the round progresses, unbutton one button after another, to expose yet more of your massive chest hair and obvious virility. If the round isn't going your way and further intimidation is needed, take off your shirt entirely. As your opponents consider the powerhouse of a man they are up against, slowly rip apart your shirt—eating and swallowing it, piece by piece.

▶ **Result:** Adds three strokes to opponent scores . . . they'll have trouble lining up shots if they're trembling in fear!

The Gunslinger

Install a gun rack that locks with a key into your cart. This rack is designed to hold your driver. When you unlock this sucker to bring out the big boy, you'll get the respect you deserve. Tell them your granddaddy taught you to treat your driver with the same respect he treated the sniper rifle he used to help defeat the foes of liberty back in World War II. Polish it. Eye it up and down the shaft. Better yet, take it to a gunsmith beforehand and have him install a real ballistic device. Fire a warning shot on the first tee to silence any nearby chirping birds. Your game will be enjoyed in respectful silence from opponents, too.

▶ **Result:** Adds one stroke to opponent scores. Two if they scream like girls when you fire your warning shot.

Protect Your Turf

Leash a hungry bulldog to the flag pole on the 18th hole so he guards a circular area around the cup. Leave just enough lead to make putting from outside this perimeter impressively difficult. Just in case you have any great long-distance putters among your competition, train Fido to gulp up any golf balls coming his way. If you don't have a dog, try tying yourself to the line, getting down on all fours, and barking territorially whenever other golfers approach the final hole. This method is especially effective when wearing a spiked collar or choke chain.

▶ **Result:** It'll be awfully hard for opponents to finish their games if they can't get close enough to putt!

Show Them the Money

Whenever you're betting on a round of golf (that is, whenever you are playing a round of golf), you want to impress upon the opposition that you have no intention of giving up your hard-earned dough without a fight. Count out the bills—no singles or fives—to cover your bet, and then, with an extra-large Bowie knife, viciously pin them to the steering wheel of your cart. Now you have shown your opponent you are good for the bet.

▶ **Result:** Increases the odds that your money stays with you—win or lose.

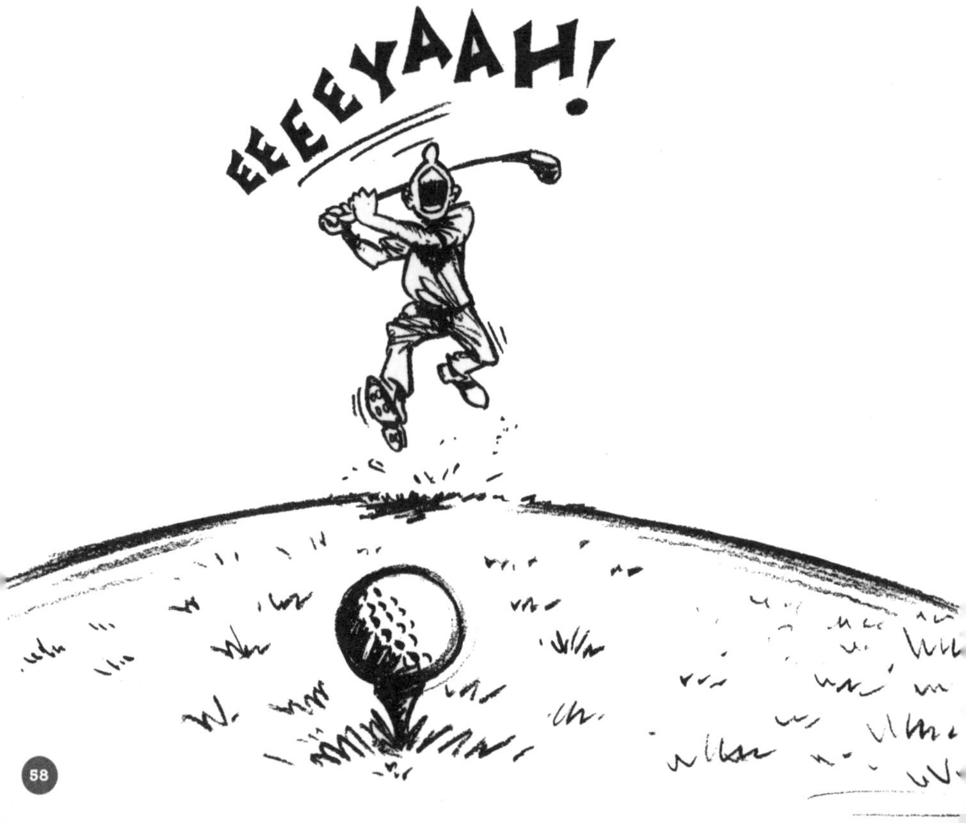
EEEEYAAH!

For Golf's Sake

Before the round, tell your buddies that the PGA is paying you to test run a new technique you've patented. On your next desperation drive (when you have nothing to lose), determinedly march off twenty paces behind the tee. Take some heaving breaths, raise your club high above your head, swing it menacingly a few times, and charge, hollering an improvised battle cry all the way. With one final grunt of exertion, take a wild sweeping hack, and hope you launch the ball into the stratosphere.

▶ **Result:** Hey, you might just get lucky. If it works, great—you'll have smacked a terrific drive and will get to enjoy the efforts of competitors trying to duplicate your success. If the ball merely takes a terrific pounding and shanks far left, they'll still admire you for your "selfless devotion" to the advancement of golf.

Contact Golf

To hell with the Stableford System or any other scoring method that involves the tedious practice of mathematics. Make up your own system of rewards and punishments. "No blood" takes on new meaning for true manly golfers—if you don't split the hole, someone's going to bleed. If you score a birdie, you are entitled to give your opponent a bloody nose. If he bogeys, you can give him one hard punch in the shoulder. Indian rubs, noogies, and other pain-provokers can be deployed at will according to score.

▶ **Result:** Weekly matches become more meaningful. You'll play better ... or else.

Section 3:

THIN THE FIELD

CLEAR THE COURSE
OF ANYONE WITH SKILL

Blow 'Em Away

Swipe a maintenance worker's uniform, an industrial-strength leaf blower, ear protectors, and dark sunglasses from the greenskeeper's shack. Stash these in your golf cart. Then if some guy in your foursome is winning decisively and needs to be taken down a step, don your uniform, hop out of your cart, and rev up the leaf blower. Whether or not there are actually leaves on the course, sweep busily toward this pretty boy each time he tries to line up for a shot. If the noise and your presence do not distract him, take more drastic action by blowing his ball into the nearest water hazard. Ignore his irate protestations; simply point to your ear guards, wave, and walk away.

▶ **Result:** Water hazard penalty for the leading golfer in your group, and the added satisfaction that you threw him off his game without ever touching his ball.

Mow 'Em Away

As in Manly Golf Tip #28, don a groundskeeper's uniform, protective ear wear, and dark sunglasses. This time, clear the field by chasing top golfers off the field on a riding lawn mower. Hone in on key competition and mow right up behind each guy like you've got important work to do and he's in your way. Follow for a while at an irritatingly close distance, and then circle and charge from the front. Repeat for all important or potentially annoying golfers on the course.

▶ **Result:** About five strokes added to key opponent scores, plus greenskeeper's gratitude for leaving the course in better shape than when you began your round.

Diverting Traffic

Keep a stack of highway traffic cones and detour signs in your cart. Race ahead of any torturously slow foursomes and reroute the cart path back into the parking lot. Pace them far enough apart to give you time to race between segments so you can stand there and indifferently wave them along without explanation. Make sure you have enough cones to redirect all slowpoke granny golfers off of a nearby cliff. Meanwhile, you'll finish your round in record time.

▶ **Result:** Doesn't necessarily subtract any strokes from your score, but easily knocks ninety minutes off the time you projected it would take to golf that day.

Brewer's Droop

Insist on a walking match with each player carrying a case of 16-ounce beers to be consumed by the end of the round. Enjoy your beers the night before, consuming twenty of the twenty-four cans and carefully replacing their contents with quick-drying cement. Replace them in the case so they look like new. Out on the course, generously offer to carry the full beers if your opponents carry the "empties." Then, as the match progresses, hand out real beers to opponents and pretend to slurp down the fake ones yourself. Drop these brew rocks one by one into the bottom of your top opponent's bag. While he gets progressively drunker, you'll still be sober. Also, he'll wonder why his bag is getting so damned heavy.

▶ **Result:** A sure match winner. No one can resist beer-drinking games. Your game will improve as you watch your opponent's game disintegrate.

My Caddy, My Bouncer

A caddy who knows his golf can provide you with invaluable course knowledge, spelling the difference between winning and losing. Then again, a guy who is 6'5", 375 lbs., shaves his head daily, has never played golf in his life, and knows nothing about course etiquette can also make for a fine selection of "caddy." He can be ready at any time to remove unwanted obstacles (skilled opponents) from the game. Before you tee off, explain to the fellows that your man "Scar" has an explosive temper, but so long as no one betters your score, everything should be cool. Have Scar make remarks to your opponents like, "Where I come from, a guy like you could be traded for two packs of menthols and a Hershey bar."

▶ **Result:** Many of us golf to escape stress. Guys like Scar create it. Add five strokes to opponent scores.

Let the Good Times Roll

Instead of a golf cart, drive a one-ton industrial steamroller onto the course. Use it to expertly flatten balls and spike marks and to groove a nifty line down the green for long benders. A steamroller can sink a foot-deep trench in a damp morning green, which makes putting an experience much like bumper-bowling. Steamrollers are useful in "accidentally" flattening opponent balls and their mouthy owners.

▶ **Result:** Improves your score by five strokes and enhances your landscaping abilities tremendously.

This Stud's for You

Golf carts are for pansies! To be a true manly golfer, hire a behemoth Clydesdale horse for the day (you know, like the ones from the beer ads). Mount your tremendous steed with polo (rather than golf) club in hand. Then play your entire game at a full gallop, paying no attention to lining up shots, or even to your score. Watch other golfers scramble out of the way at the thunderous sound of your stallion's approaching hoofbeats! This technique brings new meaning to the concept of "playing through."

▶ **Result:** OK, so your score will be terrible, but this could still be the quickest, and the coolest, round of golf in your entire life!

Get Medieval

To get in a quick round of Sunday golf, wear a suit of armor to the course and repeatedly hit into the group in front of you. When they threaten to kick your ass, call them girly men and let them rain ineffective blows upon you with their clubs until they're wheezing and too weak to move. Laugh maniacally, play through, and repeat with the next group.

▶ **Result:** By the end of the season, you'll drop eight strokes from your handicap. It's simple: The faster you play, the more you play, and the more you play, the better you get. In the long run, a suit of armor will be more beneficial than many hours spent on the practice range.

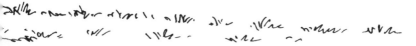

Section 4:

WHEN ALL ELSE FAILS...

OTHER TRICKS AND DIVERSIONS

Swamp Thing

Hollow out a club, and stealthily slip into a deep lake the next time you go looking for your ball. Use the hollow club as a snorkel and avoid detection by your group. After a little bit of searching, they may mourn your death, but eventually they'll move on. (A round of golf is a round of golf, after all!) Later, emerge from the lake, lost ball in hand. Stride toward your gape-jawed foursome, and calmly state that they'll very much regret skipping your turn. Then resume play as if nothing out of the ordinary has occurred.

▶ **Result:** Adds at least a stroke to each opponent's score. They'll be awed by your unearthly return from the dead.

Smoke Screen

Bigger *is* Better! In life, in golf—and you bet—in cigars. Find the biggest cigar you can and light her up! The more smoke, the better. In fact, the biggest, smokiest cigar on the planet will elevate your game to PGA levels. The goal is to create a smoke so thick and impenetrable you'll be able to play your game like you and your ball are invisible. This is especially helpful around the greens, where you can kick balls out of sand traps, improve lies, and move balls into gimme range all from within your cloak of smoke.

▶ **Result:** Subtracts four strokes from your score—and four years from your life.

Kazoo Craziness

Learn to play a mournful version of "Taps" on a kazoo and keep the instrument in your golf bag. Anytime anyone hits a ball into the water, deep into the woods, or O.B., stand ramrod straight and blast away at the heartstring-tugging number with all the air in your lungs.

▶ **Result:** Adds who-knows-how-many strokes to your opponent's score. Kazoos are the second most annoying "musical" instrument in the world. No one can stand them. Add two more strokes if you can learn the same routine using a bagpipe, which is the most annoying instrument.

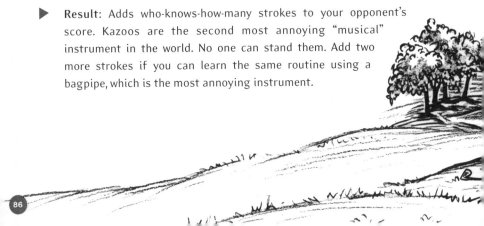

Explosive Club Toss

Nobody likes to golf with someone who loses his cool. Use this law of nature to your advantage and learn to perfect the art of "going ballistic." On your next missed putt, coldly warn your putter that there will be dire consequences the next time it disobeys your wishes. Then, if another putt misses, fly into a frothing rage and pull a stick of dynamite from your back pocket. Duct-tape it to your putter, light the sucker from your cigar, and give it a solid toss.

▶ Result: You'll have enjoyed a satisfying burst of stress relief and your opponents will think twice before testing your temper.

Das Butt

Start a discussion about your favorite submarine movies to get everyone in the mood. Then when you've smoked your cigar down to its bitter end, crouch behind a nearby ball washer and lift the knob-handled cylinder. Turn your golf cap backwards and peer through the ball hole with one eye, barking, "Torpedo room! . . . Ready! . . . Aim! . . . Fire!" Whip the smoking butt at anyone who birdied the previous hole.

▶ Result: Adds three strokes to your top opponent's score. He will become so upset at getting hit by a butt, he'll be wide open to getting his own butt kicked on the course.

Let the Big Dawg Eat

You'd be surprised to find how easy it is to get a rottweiler, German shepherd, or pit bull from your local pound. For these purposes, you'll want a dog that is rabid, hungry, or both rabid and hungry. Put your clubs in the seat next to you, and chain your new best friend to the area designed to hold your bag, at the back of the cart. As you step up to the tee, if anyone makes the mistake of saying, "Let the big dog eat!," go right up to him, look him in the eye, and say, "Are you absolutely sure about that?"

▶ **Result:** Most golfers think a four-foot putt for par is "nerve-wracking." Give them a 120-pound man-eater to think about, and their games will be destroyed. Add six strokes to their scores.

Child's Play

Golf brings out the playful side in most men. Let it bring out the child in you, the one everyone wants to slap. Spend one hole repeating, like a parrot, every single thing your opponent says. If someone says enough's enough and you should quit, throw a tantrum and say, "You're not the boss of me!" If anyone in your foursome hits a stray tee shot that trickles into the tall grass, bark like a dog "Ruff! Ruff! Ruff!" the entire way down the fairway until the player reaches his ball. If at any point during your barking he calls you immature, pee on his foot.

▶ **Result:** Adds five strokes to your opponent's score since he is likely out golfing to escape precisely the sort of behavior you're giving him.

HERE LIES
MITCH
"MY BUDDY"

Dearly Departed

After the last of your group has putted out on the 18th, and before you go to settle up the bets, ask the guys for a moment of silence. With head bowed, reach into your bag for some flowers and scatter them, along with a few tees, near the final flag. When they ask you what the hell you're doing, let them know, in a voice choked with emotion, "Mitch was the best golfing buddy I ever had. This flag marks his final resting place. I do this in remembrance of him so I can never forget." Pause dramatically here, and then howl, "Oh, how could I have done him in, all over a lousy ten-dollar bet?"

▶ **Result:** Adds about $20 in unspent bet money to your daily golf budget.

Rules Are Rules

Insist on a "play-it-where-it-lies" match and then deliberately duff a drive into a small, gentle creek. Ignore your opponent's taunts and gamely wade in and swat the ball, all the while saying you understand and obey the rules. Later, when your buddy hits one into a deep lake, simply smile and say, "Rules are rules."

▶ Result: Your opponent will lose at least five strokes and a whole lot of dignity.

BOB, YOUR GREAT ROUND OF GOLF IS ABOUT TO COME TO AN END. HOW DO I KNOW THIS? I KNOW THIS BECAUSE I HAVE BEEN WATCHING YOU. I SEE YOU WHEN Y...

Have a Gas

Two nights before an important match, sprinkle insulting comments and/or cryptic curses in gasoline around the course in places your opponents are sure to find them. Try lines like "Turn back or feel my WRATH!" or "Didn't think you'd make it here, BOB" or "The gods are very displeased." The messages won't turn up right away, but when tee time rolls around, no amount of turf maintenance will be able to remove the chemical burns. Even if the sod is replaced, the new grass likely will be a different shade than the surrounding grass, and the message should remain for weeks on end.

▶ **Result:** The groundskeeper will kill you, but it may be worth it in exchange for many laughs and a few strokes added to your rattled opponent's score.

Airborne Assault

First, learn how to skydive with pinpoint accuracy. Then set a tee time with your golf buddies and tell them you'll meet them at the first tee. Call the pro shop and insist that you will be there on time to join your party. Make sure they have your bag ready at the first tee, but have your driver, one tee, and one ball with you. Then secure a parachute and dive plane, and on the day of the match have the pilot circle over the golf course until you are dangerously close to missing your appointment. Finally, make a grand entrance—right on time!—by careening out of the sky, golf club in hand, ready to play. Execute a smooth landing near the first tee, unstrap your parachute, and calmly blast your opening drive down the fairway without so much as a practice swing.

▶ **Result:** Will impress the hell out of anyone nearby.

Mind Control

Tell your foursome that you have been studying mind control, and that your talents are progressing rapidly. When they laugh, tell them to heed your words or they will surely feel your mental wrath. Your next move will be to single out the most simpleminded member of your foursome. When no one is looking, remove his putter, put a nasty bend in it over your knee, and return it to his bag. When he next goes for his putter, he'll undoubtedly complain to the group—but everyone will deny the deed. Be sure to say to him, "I did not touch your putter . . . *with my hands.*" As he gets ready to putt, go into a deep mental trance and begin muttering strange phrases under your breath. This will throw the simpleton off his game completely, while the rest of your foursome will spend the remainder of the match wondering how far your mental powers really go.

▶ **Result:** Golf is a mental game. If you can convince your opponents you have a superior, possibly supernatural mind, you've won before you even take a swing.

Mission Impossible

Before each and every shot, address the ball as if it were a scared soldier and you were General Patton. Tell it how to behave and how important the mission is to you and all the folks back home. If you're faced with a particularly long carry over water, warn the ball that it might not make it back.

▶ **Result:** They may think you're crazy, but they'll be too awed not to salute—especially when you wallop the ball with authority.

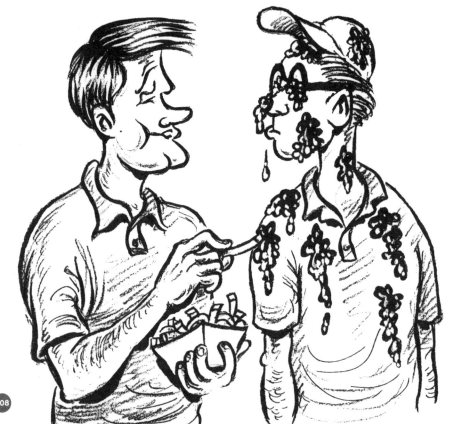

Gentlemen, Prepare Your Condiments

At the halfway house, secretly strap a dozen bungee cords to your opponent's cart and the condiment counter. After picking up your order, rev your golf cart like it's a hot rod and challenge him to race to the next tee. Ready, set, GO! He'll spend the next fifteen minutes apologizing and cleaning up spilled ketchup, relish, onions, and mustard. This leaves you with the option of either playing on and assessing him a two-stroke slow-play penalty or really rubbing it in by merely waiting at the next tee with a checkered flag around your neck.

▶ **Result:** Adds four strokes and $12 in dry-cleaning expenses to your opponent's daily totals.

Put the Crush On

Carry a novelty ball in your pocket on days when the course is crowded, and play a leisurely round at a pace that makes you most comfortable until the guys behind you start hollering to let them play through. Ignore their pleas. Don't even glance at them, and instead take extra time examining putts, selecting clubs, and repairing ball marks. If someone inadvertently or deliberately hits into you, surreptitiously switch balls to make it look like you're holding the one he just hit. When he approaches to apologize or, better still, to confront you, crush the dummy ball in your fist, glare, and say, "I don't like to be rushed. Now, which of you nancy boys is going to carry my bag the rest of the way?"

▶ **Result:** Subtracts three strokes from your score because you'll be playing at your own pace. Subtracts two more if you succeed in having somebody carry the weight of your bag the rest of the way.

About the Author

Chris Rodell (www.chrisrodell.com) is the only writer he knows of who's had articles appear simultaneously in *Maxim, National Enquirer, PetLife, Maximum Golf,* and *The South China Morning Post*. He is the co-author (with Allan Zullo) of *When Bad Things Happen to Good Golfers* and three different page-a-day calendars. He may not be the best golf writer, the most productive golf writer, or even the best-informed golf writer, but he is the only golf writer who lives on Arnold Palmer Drive, one half mile from Latrobe Country Club and King Arnold himself. No, he doesn't know Palmer, but their dogs were once good friends.